SHAPING OF A SELF

SHAPING OF A SELF

EDITED BY
LOUIS M. SAVARY
JANE C. CARTER
CHARLES BURKE

ST. MARY'S COLLEGE PRESS • WINONA, MINNESOTA

PHOTO CREDITS

Jerry Becker 18
Leslie Becker 49, 51, 59, 66, 74
Laurence Fink 60, 71
German Information Center 15, 20, 69
Cynthia Grey 5, 8, 23, 82
Walter Hastead: General Electric Company 16
Ettie de Laczay 3, 42, 80
Norwegian Tourist Office 28, cover, 79
Sylvia Plachy 39, 76
Shelly Rusten 6, 27, 34, 36, 55
David Sagarin 25, 32, 40, 52
Standard Oil of New Jersey 11
Swiss National Tourist Office 45
Uniroyal 85
United Nations 56, 62, 65

ACKNOWLEDGEMENTS

Ave Maria Press for an excerpt from *There is a Season* by Eugene S. Geissler. Copyright © 1969 by Ave Maria Press.

Ballantine Books for an excerpt from *Platzo and the Mexican Pony Rider* by Theodore Isaac Rubin. Copyright © 1965 by Theodore Isaac Rubin.

The British Broadcasting Corporation for an excerpt from *Einstein, the Man and his Achievement* by Otto Frisch and G.J. Whitrow. Copyright © 1967 by British Broadcasting Corp.

The Christian Century for the poem "To Daughter" by Dotty Goard. Reprinted by permission of author and publisher.

Delacorte Press for excerpt from *The Beatles Illustrated Lyrics* edited by Alan Aldridge. Copyright © 1969 Delacorte Press.

Dell Publishing Co. for an excerpt from *Soul on Ice* by Eldridge Cleaver. Copyright © 1965 by Eldridge Cleaver.

Doubleday and Co., Inc. for an excerpt from *The Other Side: An Account of My Experiences with Psychic Phenomena* by James A. Pike. Copyright © 1968 by Doubleday.

Famous Music Corporation for lyrics from "Alfie" by Burt Bacharach and Hal David. Copyright © 1966 by Famous Music Corporation.

Grasset, Paris for an excerpt from *La pitie dangereuse* by Stefan Zweig.

Harcourt, Brace and World for an excerpt from *Love Against Hate* by Karl Menninger. Copyright © 1959 by Harcourt, Brace and World.

Harper Torchbooks for an excerpt from *Homo Viator* by Gabriel Marcel. Copyright © 1962 by Harper.

Harper and Row for an excerpt from *Love Story* by Eric Segal. Copyright © 1970 by Eric Segal. Also for an excerpt from *The Phenomenon of Man* by Pierre Teilhard de Chardin. Copyright © 1965 by Harper and Row.

Kearney Company Inc. for an excerpt from *Strangers Eye-Kiss* by Ione Hill. Copyright © 1969 by Ione Hill. Used by permission of the author.

Life Magazine for an excerpt from "Toward a Communal Society" by Daniel Bell.

TABLE OF CONTENTS

PREFACE

No one is born into the world with a fully developed personality. We must unfold and grow in a process similar to all other living things. Just as a flower gradually responds to the heat and light of the sun, we respond to the warmth of love. As we get older and our ability to respond to others increases, we become richer persons and begin to reach greater maturity. Such development gives us a security that allows us to become unique individuals with poise and confidence. We gain a freedom that allows us to blossom into highly creative persons.

In his famous book, *Toward a Psychology of Being,* Dr. Abraham H. Maslow examines the process of personality development. Although no attempt has been made in *Shaping of a Self* to present a detailed or complete expression of Maslow's theory of personality much of the underlying thought is the same. Each part of the book presents some aspect of the growth pattern that goes from closedness to openness, from insecurity to creative maturity.

Shaping of a Self offers a rich mixture of photographs, poems and prose writings for the reader to explore and return to in moments of personal reflection. Each individual will have his unique experiences in life to compare with the insights presented here.

PART 1

THE INNER SELF

Each of us begins his life history with an *inner core* of natural instincts, needs and capacities, open to growth. This inner core is like raw material which will be shaped by forces outside us. It is delicate and easily affected by fear and disapproval, but it will never be entirely overcome or destroyed. The inner core of self has some traits that are common to all people (like the ability to love) and some that are unique to the individual (such as Paul McCartney's musical talents). Our inner core also contains unconscious aspects that may be actively repressed (for example, a fear one might have of "falling apart") or passively suppressed (as one does when he controls his fear of displaying improper table manners).

There are different ways of describing the *inner core* that gives us our uniqueness, our individual personality. Freud compared it to an iceberg — most of the iceberg is hidden in the sea and only a small portion rises above the surface to be seen. Others have taken this comparison and changed it to the view we have of a swimmer far out from shore.

The shaping of the self begins with the exploration of one's inner core. Personal discovery of forces and drives deep within the self is the key to the fascinating experience of genuine self identity. It leads us into the rich and challenging world of the hidden self. Such exploration is full of possibilities, yet our greatest happiness comes when we discover our true self, our own uniqueness.

LIKE A FLOATING HEAD

Out of these various hypotheses of Freud's, subsequently confirmed by psychiatrists all over the world, there developed the concept that only a small part of man's personality lies above the surface of consciousness and by far the greater part lies hidden. Like a distant swimmer who might appear, to a baby on the shore, as merely a floating head, there is more to us than meets the eye. Indeed, the swimmer's head wouldn't be there at all were it not for his powerful muscles moving continuously and invisibly below the surface.

Fritz Redlich
The Inside Story

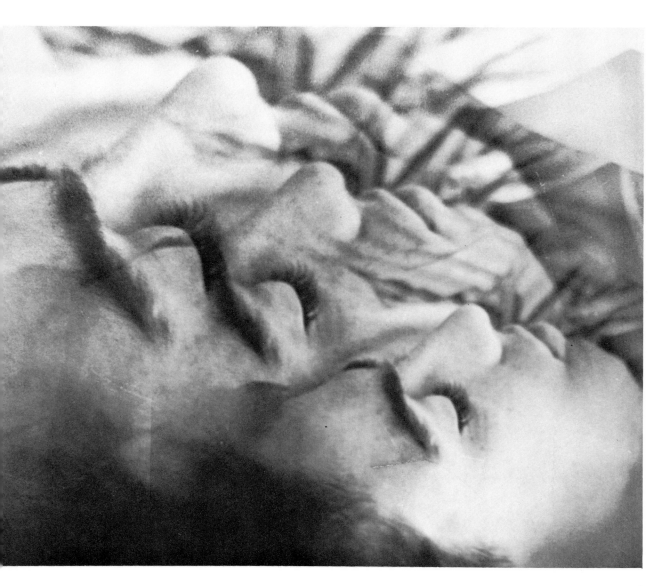

3

IT'S FREE

It's free
It is tuitionless and undiscriminatory.
It has sharp points and smooth corners.
It smells and feels and sounds and is.
It is all colors and everywhere.
It forces thinking by never explaining itself.
It is why every boy was born
and what he was born for.
It is learning.
When a light goes on in a human mind,
who has flicked the switch?
When that switch is on, what will keep it on?
What happens then?
Where will it lead?
Is it limitless?—this magical process
that is
Discovery

Geoffrey Frost
Pace

STARTING AT AGE 5

There is no absurdity so palpable
but that it may be firmly planted
in the human head
if you only begin to inculcate it
before the age of five,
by constantly repeating it
with an air of great solemnity.

Arthur Schopenhauer

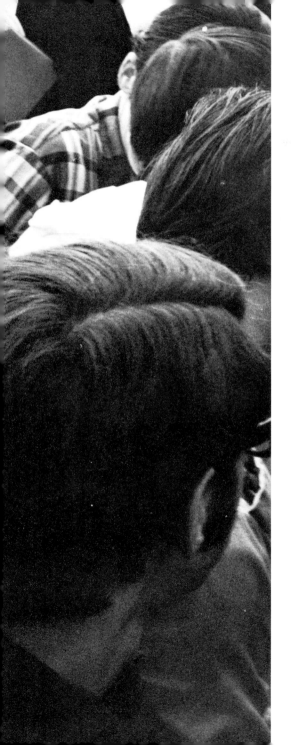

ONLY SAYING "YES"

I've never really done anything
to create what has happened.
It creates itself.
I'm here because it happened.
But I didn't do anything
to make it happen
apart from saying "Yes."

Ringo Starr

9

A THOUSAND POSSIBILITIES

At every moment you choose yourself. But do you choose your self? Body and soul contain a thousand possibilities out of which you can build many I's. But in only one of them is there a congruence of the elector and the elected. Only one—which you will never find until you have excluded all those superficial and fleeting possibilities of being and doing with which you toy, out of curiosity or wonder or greed, and which hinder you from casting anchor in the experience of the mystery of life, and the consciousness of the talent entrusted to you which is your I.

Dag Hammarskjold
Markings

10

PART 2

THE GROWING SELF

If we are to grow, we need love and respect both from ourselves and others. We must gain the confidence that allows us to unfold from within as free and mature persons. Most people will grow to health and self fulfillment through satisfaction of their basic needs. Although strength is gained in experiencing some frustration in life, too much suppression of our deepest needs can be stifling. We must grow and blossom as free persons, and not be choked by pressures and restraints on every side.

Each of us has the ability to reason and reflect. We can not only say "hello," but we know that we are saying "hello," and we know that we know this. Yet, this human ability, while it enables a person to grow, can also inhibit growth. Too much concentration on the effect we have on others can make a person a phony. The search for meaning is painful, the scene can be a litter of bitter memories, mistakes, blindness, and fear. To balance the negative experiences of life, we must have the faith of the contemporary musician who hopes that somehow through his music a miracle will happen, "which will make the blind see. . . ."

A rich mix of human experiences brings to the surface the true self in each of us. The healthy person is always hungry for growth, eager to assimilate new experiences and satisfy the needs and desires of his inner core. Yet each of us must guard against losing ourselves in activity and thus avoiding the development of genuine self identity.

"I MAKE MYSELF"

To the classic question of identity—
"Who are you?"—
a traditional person would answer:
"I am the son of my father."
But today a person says,
"I am I.
I come out of myself,
and in choice and action
I make myself."

Daniel Bell

THE HUMAN SPECIALTY

Supermen are superthinkers; anything else is a side issue. I'll allow the possibility of super-somethings which might exterminate or dominate mankind other than by outsmarting him in his own racket—thought. But I deny that it is possible for a *man* to conceive in discrete terms what such a super-something would be or how this something would win out. New Man will beat out homo sap in homo sap's own specialty—rational thought, the ability to recognize data, store them, integrate them, evaluate correctly the result, and arrive at a correct decision. That is how man got to be champion; the creature who can do it better is the coming champion. Sure, there are other survival factors, good health, good sense organs, fast reflexes, but they aren't even comparable, as the long, rough history of mankind has proved over and over—Marat in his bath, Roosevelt in his wheelchair, Caesar with his epilepsy and his bad stomach, Nelson with one eye and one arm, blind Milton; when the chips are down it's *brain* that wins, not the body's tools.

Robert A. Heinlein
"Gulf"

17

I AM NOT A CLOUD

I am not a cloud
That must be raindanced daily,
Nor a mountain to be climbed
Because I'm there.

I am a rainbow
That happens sometimes
In your light.

Ione Hill

19

20

AN ESSENCE WHICH EMANATES

Truth is an essence. An essence does not change. It emanates . . . . Any man or any woman can have it inside them as a result of their own private war within themselves. It's not just the college they fight, not just society. That's just a sideline we're trying to improve. They are fighting themselves. And if they win some of those battles, there comes an essence which by the nature of life emanates. The way a good tree pollenates and you get other good trees. The airwaves take it out. And you have the ingredients to do something that the world sees. You'll have met people who emanate this thing. It's old-fashioned. It's hard work. It can be hell. But do these kids discard it?

Patrick McGoohan

THE ROOT OF THE CRISIS

Our society is in crisis
not because we intensely disagree,
but because we feebly agree.

Abraham J. Heschel

EASIER TO MAKE REVOLUTION?

Men will sacrifice their lives
to bring about a better world
whatever that may be—
but they will not budge an inch
to attain paradise.
Nor will they struggle
to create a bit of paradise
in the hell they find themselves in.
It is much easier and gorier,
to make revolution.

Henry Miller

22

HOPE IS IMPLICIT

Confusion reigns. Truth and honesty are at a premium. A valid way of life is sought. To this end, the young explorer rolls across a wide spectrum of subject matter and musical means and mannerism. He experiments with ideology and sounds, often shaping answers in the process. Though his protest and comment are less centralized than his (black) soul brother's, [the white musician's] objective is much the same. Hope is implicit in the negation of past and present mistakes — the hope for an apocalypse, which will make the blind see, the intractable feel, the world's fearful face change.

Burt Korall
"The Music of Protest"

THE EFFECT ON OTHERS

From the moment that I become preoccupied about the effect that I want to produce on the other person, my every act, word and attitude loses its authenticity.

Gabriel Marcel

26

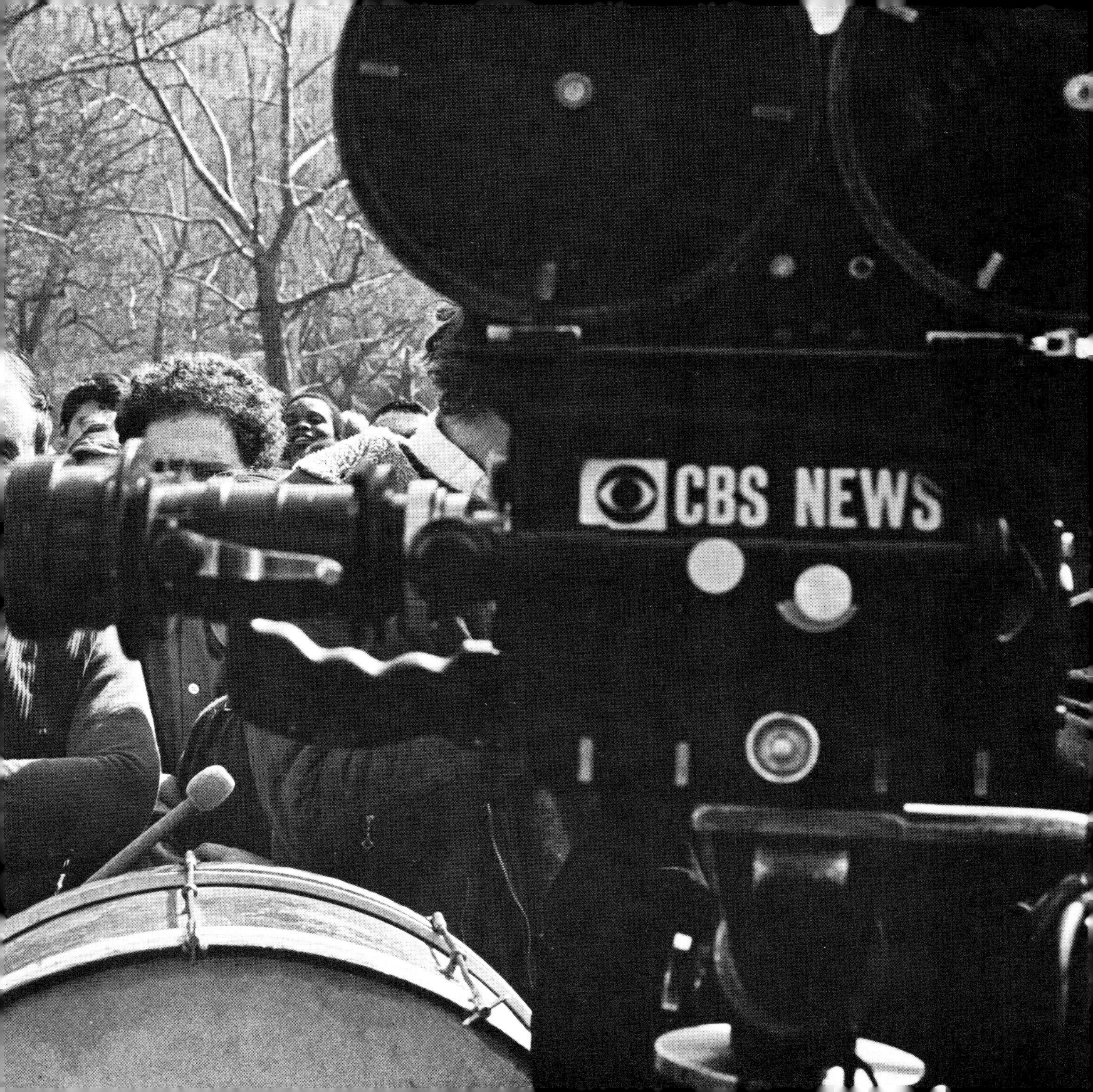
CBS NEWS

28

THE UNTRAVELLED WORLD

I am a part of all that I have met;
Yet all experience is an arch wherethro'
Gleams that untravelled world whose margin fades
For ever and for ever when I move.
How dull it is to pause, to make an end,
To rust unburnished, not to shine in use!
As tho' to breathe were life. . .

Alfred Lord Tennyson
"Ulysses"

PART 3

THE LOVING SELF

Growth always involves pain, as well as reward and pleasure. It often means giving up a simpler and easier life for one that is more demanding and responsible. Love focused on oneself must give way to more other-directed love. As Abraham Maslow puts it, our love must become self-transcending—it must become self-actualizing love.

Life can be frightening to a young person growing up in a world of mistrust and disbelief. There are many Alfies who eventually find their selfish existence unbearable. Yet not all will be fortunate enough to receive good advice from those they turn to. Some will be received warmly and will be given the strength and encouragement they seek. Others will be left with half-truths and shallow insights.

True love is not the plaything of just any beautiful or sexually stimulating experience that comes along. It is a rich and multi-faceted experience that is unique to each of us. Undoubtedly we can all recall moments in our lives when *love* has been the only word that could describe the experience we found ourselves caught up in. The glow on the faces of newly-weds radiates this deep sharing as does the playfulness of young lovers strolling through blossom scented parks in May. The first time we went out of ourselves to reach another—that was love. The shy glance, the hesitant touch, the guarded phrase—each was an attempt to express the inexpressable.

ALFIE
by Burt Bacharach & Hal David

What's it all about, Alfie,
Is it just for the moment we live?
What's it all about,
When you sort it out, Alfie,
Are we meant to take more than we give,
Or are we meant to be kind?

And if only fools are kind, Alfie,
Then I guess it is wise to be cruel,
And if life belongs
Only to the strong,
What will you mend on an old, golden rule?

As sure as I believe
There's a Heaven above, Alfie,
I know there's something much more,
Something even non-believers
Can believe in:

I believe in love, Alfie,
Without true love, we just exist, Alfie,
Until you find love
You've missed, you're nothing, Alfie . . .

When you walk let your heart lead the way,
And you'll find love any day, Alfie.

34

TO DAUGHTER

Wear your satin slippers, take my pearls;
hold still while I do your other hand;
don't forget to memorize the top ten;
mention Aristotle, Kierkegaard or Sartre;
a thing of beauty is a joy forever—Keats, not Shelley, Keats;
keys to the cottage! of course not,
    don't be silly,
well, only if you have to
but for god sakes
    don't tell your father,
God!
    Don't tell your Father.

Dotty Goard

35

THE GIRL WHO HAD RUN AWAY

A girl came to my room yesterday. She was 16 and had run away from home. Nobody had told her how wide life was. They had told her it was all over at 21. Then you're supposed to start working and stop living.

Well, this girl was 16 and she didn't want to die when she got to be 21. I told her to go on back home. That the word was out that none of us have to die if we don't want to.

I can talk like that to the kids, but who's going to tell the parents?

Donovan Leitch

37

HOW IT IS WITH LOVE

Love is a strange thing,
and how easily we lose the warm flame of it!
The flame is lost, and the smoke remains.
The smoke fills our hearts and minds,
and our days are spent in tears and bitterness.
The song is forgotten,
and the words have lost their meaning;
the perfume has gone,
and our hands are empty.
We never know how to keep the flame clear of smoke,
and the smoke always smothers the flame.
But love is not of the mind,
it is not in the net of thought,
it cannot be sought out, cultivated, cherished;
it is there when the mind is silent
and the heart is empty of the things of the mind.

J. Krishnamurti

38

WORDS THEY HAVE CHOSEN

"Are you two ready?" asked Mr. Blauvelt.

"Yes," I said for both of us.

"Friends," said Mr. Blauvelt to the others, "we are here to witness the union of two lives in marriage. Let us listen to the words they have chosen to read on this sacred occasion."

The bride first. Jenny stood facing me and recited the poem she had selected. It was very moving, perhaps especially to me, because it was a sonnet by Elizabeth Barrett:

"When our two souls stand up erect and strong,
Face to face, silent, drawing nigh and nigher
Until the lengthening wings break into fire . . ."

From the corner of my eye I saw Phil Cavilleri, pale, slack-jawed, eyes wide with amazement and adoration combined. We listened to Jenny finish the sonnet, which was in its way a kind of prayer for

"A place to stand and love in for a day

With darkness and the death hour rounding it."

Then it was my turn. It had been hard finding a piece of poetry I could read without . . . blushing. I mean, I couldn't stand there and recite lace-doily phrases. I couldn't. But a section of Walt Whitman's *Song of the Open Road,* though kind of brief, said it all for me:

"I give you my hand
I give you my love more precious than money
I give you myself before preaching or law
Will you give me yourself?
Will you travel with me?
Shall we stick by each other as long as we live?

I finished, and there was a wonderful hush in the room. Then Ray Stratton handed me the ring, and Jenny and I—ourselves—recited the marriage vows, taking each other as husband and wife, from that day forward, to love and cherish, 'til death do us part.

Eric Segal
Love Story

41

42

WHERE SHE HAS GONE

Though I am old with wandering
Through hollow lands and hilly lands,
I will find out where she has gone,
And kiss her lips and take her hands;
And walk among long dappled grass,
And pluck till time and times are done
The silver apples of the moon,
The golden apples of the sun.

W.B. Yeats
from "The Song of Wandering Aengus"

THE MARRIAGE OF TRUE MINDS

Let me not to the marriage of true minds
Admit impediments. Love is not love
Which alters when it alteration finds,
Or bends with the remover to remove:
O, no! it is an ever-fixed mark
That looks on tempests and is never shaken;
It is the star to every wandering bark,
Whose worth's unknown, although his height be taken.
Love's not Time's fool, though rosy lips and cheeks
Within his bending sickle's compass come:
Love alters not with his brief hours and weeks,
But bears it out even to the edge of doom.
If this be error and upon me proved,
I never writ, nor no man ever loved.

William Shakespeare

44

PART 4

THE SEARCHING SELF

Healthy people enjoy using their capacities, talents, and physical powers. It is a delight for them to find a challenge and overcome it. They enjoy the feeling of growth that results from having expanded their horizons a bit more by solving a new problem or working through a difficult and unknown situation. Such people are motivated by a strong desire to transcend their previous limits; they seek to be self-actualizing and expansive persons.

The uneasiness of finding oneself in contemporary society is indeed common to us all. So many life-styles are thrust upon us, so many causes are put before us. Which combination is best for me? Which path will lead to genuine self-discovery? What roles draw me merely because they satisfy a personal deficiency? Maturity is not easily reached by anyone. Self-fulfillment is a life-long adventure.

Nevertheless, it is possible to grow out of ourselves and to become richer persons in the process. The first experiences of love give us courage to reach out little by little. Soon we learn that personal security is strengthened by the loving risks that we freely choose to take. Maturity and self-fulfillment are obviously linked with our capacity to love.

The mature, self-actualizing person learns his true worth and rests secure in the confidence that such knowledge brings. He can no longer be threatened by superficial losses of material goods or physical attributes. His strength lies in his personal self-acceptance. This no man can take from him.

"EMPTY SKINS, PLASTIC SHELLS"

I can see them all
Not just one group, one style
But all groups, all styles
Cramped in their grooves
Staring, glaring, rushing, screaming
"Be like me, be like me!"
Types neat and impotent
Lost and searching
Secure and dead
Mod and empty
You can get so confused
Empty skins, plastic shells
Disposable
Expecting you to be something
But all forgetting life
Loving just to live
Being real people
Think again
Has all honesty gone under
Drowned in a war
You lost?

Pace essay

48

A QUESTION OF STYLE

To be born to create, to love to win at games is to be born to live in time of peace. But war teaches us to lose everything and become what we were not. It all becomes a question of style.

Albert Camus

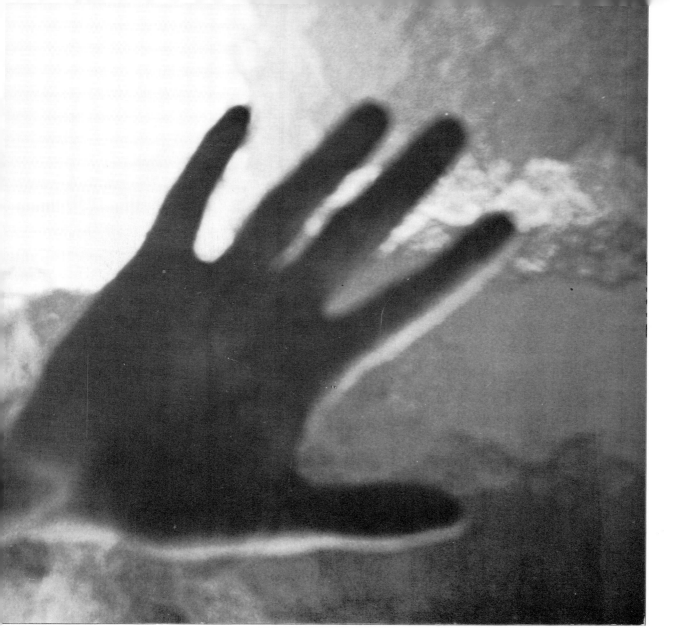

52

WITHOUT ANY OTHER CONTINUITY

I lived consequently without any other continuity than that, from day to day, of I, I, I. From day to day women, from day to day virtue or vice, from day to day, like dogs—but every day myself secure at my post. Thus I progressed on the surface of life, in the realm of words as it were, never in reality. All those books barely read, those friends barely loved, those cities barely visited, those women barely possessed! I went through the gestures out of boredom or absent-mindedness. Then came human beings; they wanted to cling, but there was nothing to cling to, and that was unfortunate—for them. As for me, I forgot. I never remembered anything but myself.

Albert Camus
The Fall

WHAT HE EXPECTED

The conflict between his desires and his fears was obvious. He wanted to love—but he feared the consequences. Instead of expecting love in return, he expected a cold and uncaring response. What, by and large, he saw around him only confirmed his suspicion that "that's the way people are." As much as I might wish he could see things more positively, I knew he could not simply erase his experiences or his observation.

James A. Pike
The Other Side

A WORLD OF FIRE AND DEW

I would mould a world of fire and dew
With no one bitter, grave, or over wise,
And nothing marred or old to do you wrong . . .
Where beauty has no ebb, decay no flood,
But joy is wisdom, time an endless song.

W.B. Yeats
from "The Land of Heart's Desire"

A LEAP INTO THE UNKNOWN

I place a great deal of emphasis on people really listening to each other, to what the other person has to say, because you very seldom encounter a person who is capable of taking either you or himself seriously. Of course, when I was out of prison I was not really like this; the seeds were there, but there was too much confusion and madness mixed in. I had a profound desire for communicating with and getting to know other people, but I was incapable of doing so. I didn't know how.

Getting to know someone, entering that new world, is an ultimate, irretrievable leap into the unknown. The prospect is terrifying. The stakes are high. The emotions are overwhelming. The two people are reluctant really to strip themselves naked in front of each other, because in doing so they make themselves vulnerable and give enormous power over themselves one to the other. How often they inflict pain and torment upon each other! Better to maintain shallow, superficial affairs; that way the scars are not too deep. No blood is hacked from the soul.

Eldridge Cleaver
Soul on Ice

TODAY I AM A TURBINE

Today I am a turbine, strong and with no edges. I am swift. I am smooth. I am unbreakable. I roll about my room and shout I am a turbine, a strong durable turbine and all my strength, my steel turbine strength stays within me. Like a ball it goes around in me and none gets out and I remain strong and give none of my hissing, sizzling power to the outside of me.

I leave the house of my family, my upright, rectangular, non-rounded family. I leave to steam along a straight-lined squared street and only I am round among the many edges, the sharp edges, the sharp-edged people . . .

When they look at me I smile. To myself I smile. To myself I shout. With a ball of happiness in my deep round chest my shouting laugh bounces up and around in my unbreakable steel heart. They glide off me. Their smiles, their speech, their looks, their touch, their many-edged barbs glide from my round, smooth, strong surface. They can not hurt me and I will not be hurt for I know that the steel ball that is me can not be entered.

Coils and coils of steel wrapped tight layer upon layer leaving no space and no weakness, each layer full of power and giving power to its next powerful neighbor and all of it me. Me, I walk and talk and edges see me and if they shove me, if they hurt me, I shall say and do nothing. They only hurt Arthur Turbitzky, an outer shell, an outer edge, and inside a turbine laughs with the knowledge of coils of power that can strike dead and demolish whole populations of edges. I, a turbine whose energy is well governed, systematized and really uncaring.

Theodore Isaac Rubin
Platzo and the Mexican Pony Rider

62

IDENTITY AND SELFLESSNESS

It has also been discovered
that precisely those persons
who have the clearest and strongest identity
are exactly the ones
who are most able to transcend
the ego or the self
and to become selfless,
who are at least relatively selfless
and relatively egoless.

Abraham H. Maslow

A CHANGE OF MIND

Although I often saw Einstein,
I met him only briefly.
The quality that dominated his personality
was a very great and genuine modesty.
When anyone contradicted him
he thought it over
and if he found he was wrong
he was delighted,
because he felt that he had escaped from an error
and that now he knew better.
For the same reason he never hesitated
to change his opinion
when he found that he had made a mistake,
and to say so.
There was an occasion when somebody accused him
of saying something different
from what he had said a few weeks previously,
and Einstein replied,
"Of what concern is it to the dear Lord
what I said three weeks ago!"

Otto Frisch

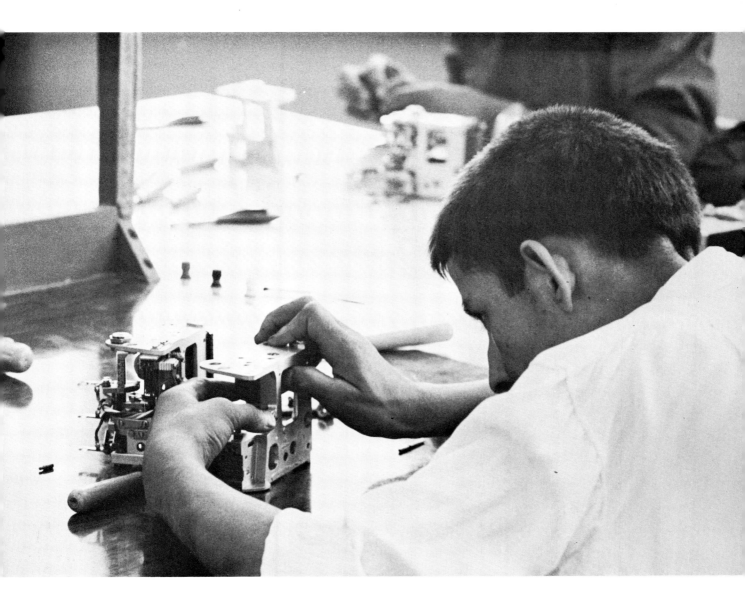

LISTENING

Listening is a magnetic and strange thing, a creative force. The friends who listen to us are the ones we move toward, and we want to sit in their radius. When we are listened to, it creates us, makes us unfold and expand.

I discovered this a few years ago. Before that, when I went to a party I would think anxiously: "Now try hard. Be lively." But now I tell myself to listen with affection to anyone who talks to me. This person is showing me his soul. It is a little dry and meager and full of grinding talk just now, but soon he will begin to think. He will show his true self; will be wonderfully alive.

Karl Menninger
Love Against Hate

TWO KINDS OF PITY

There are two kinds of pity.
One is weak and sentimental,
and is really merely
the heart's impatience
to rid itself as soon as possible
of the painful emotion
elicited by another's suffering.
This has nothing to do with compassion;
it is an instinctive defense of the soul
against external suffering.

And the other pity,
the only one that matters,
is not sentimental but creative.
It knows what it wants
and is determined to hold fast
to the extreme limit of human strength.

Stefan Zweig

TO BE HUMBLE

Humility is just as much the opposite of self-abasement as it is of self-exaltation. To be humble is not to make comparisons. Secure in its reality, the self is neither better nor worse, bigger nor smaller, than anything else in the universe. It—is nothing, yet at the same time one with everything. It is in this sense that humility is absolute self-effacement.

To be nothing in the self-effacement of humility, yet for the sake of the task, to embody its whole weight and importance in your bearing, as the one who has been called to undertake it. To give to people, works, poetry, art, what the self can contribute, and to take, simply and freely, what belongs to it by reason of its identity. Praise and blame, the winds of success and adversity, blow over such a life without leaving a trace or upsetting its balance.
Towards this, so help me, God. . .

Dag Hammarskjold
Markings

PART 5

THE ACTUALIZING SELF

The self-actualizing person is always in process, he is always becoming more real. He has learned to drop the defenses of earlier childhood and has become strong and independent, no longer doing things out of fear of disapproval or anxiety but rather because he has freely chosen to do them. This new found freedom allows him to be selfless, creative, and eager to explore the world of reality outside of himself. Abraham Maslow describes the life of a self-actualizing person as being characterized by dedication to something "bigger than oneself."

While many may view the world as a place filled with "ignorant armies" of fighting men where people live lives marked by confusion and fear, others make use of such strife to become richer individuals. Melina Mercouri, the actress, is such a person. She speaks as a woman who is shaping a self, a woman who represents a cause, one who is trying to create her own future. We have all found ourselves in positions where we could grow by standing firm in our convictions or retreat in insecure self-defense because we feared the consequences. The self-actualizing person overcomes his need for social acceptance and stands firm when personal convictions are at stake.

For Camus, Hammarskjold, Teilhard, and for many others, the journey into the future is not to be made alone. A person will make the adventure with his friends and with confidence in the goal he seeks. This life adventure, this growth in self-actualization, is a continuous effort "to seek a newer world."

AS ON A DARKLING PLAIN

Ah, love, let us be true
To one another! for the world, which seems
To lie before us like a land of dreams,
So various, so beautiful, so new,
Hath really neither joy, nor love, nor light,
Nor certitude, nor peace, nor help for pain;
And we are here as on a darkling plain
Swept with confused alarms of struggle and flight,
Where ignorant armies clash by night.

Matthew Arnold

WHY MAN WAS CREATED

Hunger is my native place in the land of the passions. Hunger for fellowship, hunger for righteousness—for a fellowship founded on righteousness, and a righteousness attained in fellowship.

Only life can satisfy the demands of life. And this hunger of mine can be satisfied for the simple reason that the nature of life is such that I can realize my individuality by becoming a bridge for others, a stone in the temple of righteousness.

Don't be afraid of yourself, live your individuality to the full—but for the good of others. Don't copy others in order to buy fellowship, or make convention your law instead of living the righteousness.

To become free and responsible. For this alone was man created, and he who fails to take the Way which could have been his shall be lost eternally.

Dag Hammarskjold
Markings

76

WHAT DOES FREEDOM MEAN?

I shall have that passport back. All my life I have been pessimistic: in regard to love, to my career, to my beauty. Yet today I wave the flag of optimism. Even if it is not logical, I cannot afford the luxury of logic. I must have hope. I am another woman now. I have learned to say no. Before, I couldn't. The first tear, the first caress, made me answer: Yes. And so I changed color every five minutes. Now I have a very definite color, the color of No. Because I happened to receive a gift; that is, to understand injustice, to discover dignity. From now on, nobody will smile with me for my being frivolous and crazy and paradoxical as I used to be when I thought: Who cares, I am only an actress, they want me like this. I am going to study, to find the answers and know the words to use when I'm asked: "What is democracy? What does freedom mean?" Answering with my feelings only is not enough. Because I no longer am Melina Mercouri, actress. I am a woman who represents a cause. I did not look for such a flag, but Patakos has put it into my hands and now I hold it tight.

Melina Mercouri

PRIVATE PERSON, PUBLIC OFFICE

A man in public office is not wholly free to keep private his views on vital public matters. He must accept in principle the fact that there are times when the public good overrides personal considerations and when loyalty to party or to an office or even to a President must be relegated to a secondary position. A time when in fact, resignations with explanation are both right and necessary to the public good.

Eugene McCarthy

STRENGTH TO LIVE AS A FREE MAN

How am I to find the strength to live as a free man, detached from all that was unjust in my past and all that is petty in my present, and so, daily, to forgive myself?

Life will judge me by the measure of the love I myself am capable of, and with patience according to the measure of my honesty in attempting to meet its demands, and with an equity before which the feeble explanations and excuses of self-importance carry no weight whatsoever.

Dag Hammarskjold
Markings

80

WHITSUNDAY, 1961

I don't know Who—or what—put the question, I don't know when it was put. I don't even remember answering. But at some moment I did answer Yes to Someone—or Something—and from that hour I was certain that existence is meaningful and that, therefore, my life, in self-surrender, had a goal.

From that moment I have known what it means "not to look back," and "to take no thought for the morrow."

Led by the Ariadne's thread of my answer through the labyrinth of life, I came to a time and place where I realized that the Way leads to a triumph which is a catastrophe, and to a catastrophe which is a triumph, that the price for committing one's life would be reproach, and that the only elevation possible to man lies in the depths of humiliation. After that, the word "courage" lost its meaning, since nothing could be taken from me.

As I continued along the Way, I learned, step by step, word by word, that behind every saying in the Gospels stands one man and one man's experience. Also behind the prayer that the cup might pass from him and his promise to drink it. Also behind each of the words from the Cross.

Dag Hammarskjold
Markings

81

82

THE EXPERIENCE OF A FATHER

There is always at least a little, if not a lot more, maturity to achieve. There is always something to be added or to be refined about one's attitude to life and one's grasp of the meaning of life. Maturity is not a static state, a high plateau with no place else to go. It too is subject to the dynamism of change—in either direction. Exposed a second time to searching and deciphering the meaning of life with his teenagers, a father may well be challenged to go up higher and to see better.

Eugene S. Geissler

SEEING

Seeing. We might say the whole of life lies in that verb—if not ultimately, at least essentially. Fuller being in closer union . . . . But . . . union increases only through an increase in consciousness, that is to say in vision. And that, doubtless, is why the history of the living world can be summarized as the elaboration of ever more perfect eyes within a cosmos in which there is always something more to be seen . . . . To try to see more and better is not a matter of whim or curiosity or self-indulgence. To see or to perish is the very condition laid upon everything that makes up the universe, by reason of the mysterious gift of existence . . . . I repeat that my only aim . . . my whole driving power, is to try to see; that is to say, to try to develop a homogeneous and coherent perspective of our general experience extended to man.

A whole which unfolds.

Pierre Teilhard de Chardin

TO SEEK A NEWER WORLD

Come, my friends.
'T is not too late to seek a newer world.
Push off, and sitting well in order smite
The sounding furrows; for my purpose holds
To sail beyond the sunset, and the baths
Of all the western stars, until I die.

Alfred Lord Tennyson